Original title:
Plasma Poems

Copyright © 2025 Creative Arts Management OÜ
All rights reserved.

Author: Rosalie Bradford
ISBN HARDBACK: 978-1-80567-806-9
ISBN PAPERBACK: 978-1-80567-927-1

Currents Unseen

In a world where the giggles flow,
Electricity dances, stealing the show.
Socks on my hands, the light bulb's grins,
Even the toaster dreams of wins.

Wires whisper secrets, oh so tight,
Joking with switches, flicking left and right.
Charging my phone with a rubber duck,
Who knew that chaos could bring such luck?

Prismatic Reflections

Mirrors of color, bouncing around,
Silly shadows on the ground.
Lightbulbs wearing hats so bright,
Chasing rainbows in sheer delight.

Giggles caught in a glassy sheen,
Reflection whispers, 'This is my scene.'
Each prism a joke, a chuckle, a grin,
Who knew spectrums could wear such skin?

Vortex of Ideas

Swirling thoughts like leaves in breeze,
Creative chaos that aims to please.
Ideas pop like corn in air,
Spinning and twirling with flair.

The whirlwind laughs, a friendly tease,
Tickling minds like a gentle sneeze.
Round and round in a merry flight,
Clowns on bicycles take to the night.

The Light Within

A bulb in my brain flickers to life,
Sparks of humor, bustling with strife.
Jokes that glow and funny thoughts sing,
Bright ideas sprouting, what joy they bring.

When the world feels a bit too dim,
I flip the switch; let the laughter brim.
With energy boundless, let your heart spin,
For we all have some light tucked within.

Spectrum of Sentience

In a rainbow of thoughts, colors collide,
Where ideas like socks take wild rides.
Imagination bounces, a brilliant spree,
Who knew wisdom could look so silly?

Thoughts dance like jellybeans on a plate,
Mixing and mingling in a colorful state.
Laughter erupts with each quirky hue,
Making even Einstein chuckle anew.

Light's Embrace

A beam of wit shines bright and bold,
Tickling the shadows, stories unfold.
Glowing giggles, they flicker and flare,
Lighthearted whispers floating in air.

Sunshine tickles, a radiant tease,
Finding the humor in quirky unease.
Spinning in circles, we chase the glow,
Chasing our shadows, just let it flow.

Quicksilver Echoes

Bouncing ideas like a silver ball,
Hopping around like it's having a ball.
Chasing the echoes of laughter's thrill,
Every punchline a spark, a joyous spill.

Quick as a wink, humor takes flight,
Shimmering chatter, keeping it light.
Tickled by thoughts that swirl and sway,
Who knew echoes could dance in such a way?

Boundless Horizons

Beyond the horizon, the chuckles extend,
Where horizons meld and the laughter blends.
Each giggle a traveler, roaming so free,
Sailing the jokes like ships on a spree.

The sky's the limit; let humor take flight,
Dancing on clouds, oh what a sight!
With every horizon, the laughter will grow,
A boundless adventure, just go with the flow.

Sublime Currents

In the kitchen, sparks do fly,
With boiling soup and pie in the sky.
The toaster thinks it's a great dance,
While the kettle hums, not missing a chance.

The blender whirs with zestful glee,
Chunky salsa, oh, what a spree!
The fridge lights up with disco flair,
While brussels sprouts stop and stare.

Light bulbs flicker in rhythmic tune,
As noodles swirl like a cartoon.
Electric giggles in every space,
Watch out! The sock hops with grace!

Bananas slip, oh, what a sight,
Pasta twirls in sheer delight.
The spatula waves, it's quite a show,
In this kitchen, chaos steals the glow!

The Art of Illumination

In the dark, my lamp's a star,
It whispers secrets from afar.
With a flick, it sparkles bright,
Making shadows dance in fright.

The candle winks with melted grace,
As matches join the wild race.
A bubble of light, so keen to play,
I swear it giggled just today!

Flashlight beams like a silly clown,
Chasing shadows all around.
The toaster snaps, a pop-up show,
It never knows when to take a bow!

Neon signs hum a zesty tune,
While disco balls make the room.
This crazy dance of light and cheer,
Illuminates laughter, far and near!

Synthesis of the Stars

Twinkle, twinkle, silly star,
You shine bright, but who you are?
Falling fast with all your might,
Do you wish to start a fight?

Chasing dreams through cosmic lanes,
Hitching rides on comet trains.
Planets giggle, asteroids play,
How do you dance in such a way?

Galaxies swirl like ice cream scoops,
Laughter echoes through the troops.
Supernovas burst with cheer,
What a party—bring the beer!

Ethereal Embers

Dancing flames in the night,
Flickering with pure delight.
Ghostly sparks that wear a grin,
Making mischief, let's begin!

Whispers float on smoky air,
Giggles glow, without a care.
Why do you giggle, my dear flame?
Oh right, you're always playing games!

Ethereal jokes fill the dark,
Lighting up, just like a lark.
Every ember shares a laugh,
You trip on me, I'll take a bath!

Radiant Tides

Waves that giggle on the shore,
Tickling toes, always want more.
Sandy castles fall apart,
Who knew waves had such a heart?

Seashells sing a merry tune,
Bubbles burst like tiny balloons.
The ocean's a comedian's dream,
With splashy laughter, it does beam!

Riding ripples, slides of fun,
Splashing about 'til day is done.
Even sharks can crack a joke,
"Why so serious?" says the bloke!

The Alchemy of Light

Mixing colors, paint it bright,
Turning day into pure delight.
Joking shades of azure hue,
Why so blue? Just passing through!

Sunbeams sprinkle, laughter shines,
Creating rainbows, twisty lines.
Light giggles, bends, and prances,
Who knew photons love to dance?

With every flicker, sparks take flight,
Transforming darkness into light.
Alchemy of giggles bright,
Bringing joy with sheer delight!

Ethereal Connections

In the realm where electrons dance,
Giggles swirl in a cosmic trance.
Electrons tease, they jump and pop,
Creating sparks that never stop.

Jokes are traded like photons bright,
Bouncing laughter, a joyful sight.
In a world where whims collide,
Ethereal jokes can't be denied.

Spectrum of Sentiment

Rainbows stretch across the skies,
Witty quips and playful sighs.
Every color sings a tune,
Dancing light beneath the moon.

Grins that flicker, glances bold,
Silliness never gets too old.
From violet giggles to orange glee,
A spectrum of smiles, just you and me.

Luminous Lines

Neon scribbles, bright and wild,
Crafting laughter, like a child.
Words like fireflies, they glow,
Tickling thoughts we all should know.

In the night, they paint the air,
Witty whispers everywhere.
Each line shines, a jolly twist,
Luminous fun you can't resist.

Vibrations of Infinity

Bouncing waves of humor roll,
Tidal laughter takes its toll.
With a chuckle, we all rise,
Vibrations echo through the skies.

Cosmic giggles, in-between,
Tickles time, a silly scene.
Infinite joy, let's dive in,
With vibrant laughs, we always win.

Ethereal Currents

In a world where currents dance,
Electric thoughts begin to prance.
Like socks that vanish in the wash,
Ideas swirl, a lightning quash.

With giggles zipping through the air,
A buzz that tickles without a care.
The jokes are charged, they light the night,
Like squirrels on caffeine, taking flight!

Luminescent Whispers

Tiny sparks of whispered glee,
Glowing secrets, just for me.
They shimmer softly in the dark,
Like fireflies making their own spark.

A glow-in-the-dark dance party here,
With jokes and laughter, we persevere.
Light-hearted quips, they dance around,
In this bright realm, joy is found.

Waves of Radiance

Surfing on waves of vibrant light,
A quirky sight, a funny fright.
Banana peels and giggles collide,
As we ride the currents, let's not hide.

Splashes of laughter on every crest,
Who knew that joy could be such a jest?
Surfboards made from silly dreams,
We conquer the sea of laughter beams.

Celestial Fusion

Stars collide in a jovial scheme,
Creating a chaos that makes you beam.
With cosmic giggles swirling about,
The galaxy dances, there's no doubt.

Spaghetti comets zooming by,
With meatball moons up in the sky.
This fusion of fun takes us high,
In a universe that makes us fly!

Light in Flux

In a dance of rays, they twist and twirl,
The colors collide, becoming a swirl.
A giggling photon, lost in the fun,
What's it like? Oh, just a light-hearted run!

With a flick and a flash, they play peek-a-boo,
Tickling the dark with a bright, cheeky hue.
They race through the air, a spark of delight,
Creating a ruckus, igniting the night.

Frequency of Being

I tune in and out like a radio guest,
Finding my vibe, oh isn't it best?
A bouncy wave, with giggles galore,
Strumming the notes of existence's core.

I laugh with the bass, and waltz with the treble,
Each heartbeat a rhythm, oh what a rebel!
Dancing through life, on a silly frequency,
Twirling in circles, oh so serendipity!

Kaleidoscope of Thought

Oh what a scene when my mind's in a spin,
Flashes of colors, the laughter begins.
Ideas collide, creating a mess,
Like socks in the dryer, oh what a stress!

With each turn of shift, a new pattern takes flight,
A silly parade, a zany delight.
Thoughts bounce around, in wiggly lines,
In this jumbled world, even chaos shines!

Electric Realms

In circuits of joy, where giggles abound,
Electricity dances, making all sound.
A zap and a zing, oh what a surprise,
Like squirrels on caffeine, we jump to the skies!

Sparks of humor fly, in a shocking delight,
Jumping with glee, day turns into night.
These realms of voltage, where fun is the key,
Is it magic or science? Why not let it be!

The Glow of Creation

In a lab of bright sparks, a madman grins,
Juggling atoms, where chaos begins.
With bursts of color, and giggled delight,
He mixes the juice of the stars each night.

"Eureka!" he shouts with a pie on his face,
As he dances with energy, running the race.
His goggles askew, he fumbles and tumbles,
Creating a shimmer, as laughter now rumbles.

Connecting Waves

Two silly particles playing tag,
Bouncing and laughing with no time to lag.
"Catch me!" they whisper, swirling with glee,
As they hop through the air, wild and free.

They throw wave parties, flashing dance moves,
Twisting like noodles, oh look at them groove!
In perfect sync, they wiggle and sway,
Making all the neutrinos join in for a play!

Boundless Radiance

A shout from a photon, quick as a wink,
"I'm the brightest of all! Now go have a drink!"
With a flick and a flash, he races to show,
The wonders of light, just lost in the flow.

Particles party, no one's quite sure,
If they're liquid or solid, they giggle demure.
"Let's shine like stars!" they cheer and they beam,
In a realm where the silliness reigns supreme!

Emanations of Thought

In the mind's wild playground, ideas collide,
Thought bubbles pop as they swirl and slide.
"What if ducks wore hats and danced in the rain?"
Thoughts giggle and bounce, unchained from the mundane.

A tickle of genius, a splash of whimsy,
Spirits of laughter, oh isn't it flimsy?
From absurdity springs a great cosmic fun,
We're all just ideas, playing under the sun!

Fractals of Light

In shades of pink and yellow,
They dance like jelly on the ground.
Each turn, a twist, so quite mellow,
In this chaos, joy is found.

A swirl, a bounce, a giggle fits,
They shimmer like they've had too much.
With every step, in fits and bits,
They sparkle forth, and we all touch.

Twisting shapes and funny sights,
They twirl about like little bugs.
Life's refractive, in pure delights,
And really, who needs all those mugs?

So chase them down, those fractal beams,
With laughter that just won't subside.
In every blend, we spin our dreams,
And in this light, we all confide.

Celestial Symphony

The stars are singing off the charts,
With tones of cheese and cream delight.
The moonlight winks and plays its parts,
In this bizarre galactic night.

Jupiter hums while Saturn laughs,
As comets jazz their way around.
With every note, a giggle wafts,
In melodies that know no bounds.

A symphony of playful glee,
As stardust sparkles in the air.
The cosmos holds its wild decree,
And we, like nuts, just sit and stare.

So let us dance with twinkling lights,
In cosmic jams that make us sway.
With every beat, the universe bites,
And tickles us in wacky ways.

Pulses of the Infinite

Beats like popcorn in the void,
Jumping up with every pulse.
The rhythm makes the dark paranoid,
And spins around in great convulse.

Each thump a giggle from the stars,
Each bounce a wiggle from the sun.
The galaxies dance in funny cars,
While black holes just block out the fun.

On cosmic drums, the universe plays,
With quarks that bounce like rubber balls.
We laugh along these stellar rays,
And ride the starlight's endless calls.

In this dance of endless beats,
The cosmos cracks a cosmic grin.
And as it pulses, life repeats,
In waves that tingle from within.

Fiery Constellations

Oh, how the stars ignite and flare,
A bonfire just waiting to gleam.
With laughter swirling in the air,
They form a cosmic comical dream.

Like flames that jiggle in the breeze,
They pop and sparkle, oh so bright.
In laughter's heat, we find our ease,
As constellations giggle with light.

Orion drops his sword in jest,
And Leo's mane begins to shake.
They roast marshmallows at their best,
While shooting stars begin to bake.

So let us toast throughout the night,
With fiery friends up in the sky.
In constellation's cheeky light,
We find our joy, oh me, oh my!

Shimmering Forces

In a dance of bubbles, they rise,
Like disco balls under sunny skies.
They bounce and giggle, a bubbly crew,
Whispering secrets, just me and you.

In a flask of joy, they twirl about,
Making the scientist laugh and shout.
With every wiggle, they sing their tune,
Under the watchful eye of the moon.

When they collide, it's silly, you see,
Making faces as funny as can be.
Jellybeans in a fizzy spree,
These glowing marvels, so wild and free.

Oh, the antics of these shimmering friends,
A comedy show that never ends.
With zany leaps and whimsical grace,
They paint a smile on the grumpiest face.

Circuitry of Emotion

Wires buzzing with laughter and cheer,
Sending zaps of joy far and near.
A spark of wit lights up the night,
Connecting odd thoughts in pure delight.

When feelings flicker, oh what a sight,
A jolt of humor gives wings to flight.
Electrons giggle as they race,
In a bright and quirky, bustling space.

Comedic circuits, they twist and bend,
Crafting chuckles that never end.
With a click and a zap, they play a game,
Oh, the antics of this zany frame!

Fuses pop with a cheerful crack,
As they journey along the electric track.
Riding the highs and the silly lows,
In this crazy world where laughter flows.

Flickering Thoughts

Thoughts flicker like fireflies in the night,
Dancing in chaos, giving fright,
But when they glow with a playful spin,
Laughter erupts from deep within.

A scattered idea, a whimsical spark,
Chasing shadows from the dark.
Kooky concepts play hide and seek,
Tickling the minds that they peek.

They bounce like balloons, floating high,
Twirling and swirling, oh my, oh my!
With every flicker, a giggle starts,
Painting smirks on curious hearts.

In this circus of quirks, thoughts take flight,
Creating a spectacle, oh what a sight!
Flickering beams of joy and jest,
Inviting all to join the quest.

Charges of Inspiration

A zap of laughter fills the air,
As ideas dance without a care.
Bouncing like puppies chasing a tail,
Inspiration's journey will never fail.

With every jolt, a story unfolds,
Crafting dreams that are daring and bold.
A burst of energy, a whimsical ride,
Where imagination becomes the guide.

Charges sparking with playful might,
They twine and tease, a delight in flight.
Like a rollercoaster, round they go,
In this carnival where wonders flow.

So gather your sparks and join the fun,
In a land where the giggles have just begun.
With each new charge, let the laughter soar,
In inspiration's grip, who could ask for more?

Pulses of Light

In the realm where thoughts ignite,
Ideas bounce like stars at night.
Giggles spark from every source,
Like photons racing, on a course.

Waves of laughter, bright and bold,
Charged with fun, they're uncontrolled.
A jump, a skip, a flash of glee,
Dancing beams of jubilee.

Tickles run through every beam,
A silly joke can light a dream.
Flickering thoughts like fireflies,
Chasing shadows, watch them rise.

Let's ride this wave, don't be shy,
On beams of laughter, we will fly.
Oh, the brightness never fades,
In this light, our joy cascades.

Photon Dance

In a disco of the mind,
Dancing lights, so unconfined.
Twinkling jokes and prancing beams,
Chasing after silly dreams.

With every step, a quarky spin,
Our laughter, feathery, takes a win.
Glow sticks swirling, what a sight,
We boogie down with pure delight.

Energy zips from friend to friend,
A comedy wave that will not end.
Volts of giggles flood the room,
While silliness begins to bloom.

As photons leap, we shout hooray,
Join the dance, don't drift away.
In this rhythm, joy shall spark,
Together, we'll light up the dark.

Energy in Motion

With a twitch and a zap we go,
Silly sparks begin to flow.
Energized by laughter's twist,
Join the ride—you won't resist.

Bouncing off each cheeky grin,
A whirl of fun, let's begin.
Wattage high, we'll electrify,
Chasing echoes, oh my, oh my!

Giggles crackle, lights explode,
Joyful chaos on this road.
Every joke a jolt of surprise,
Together we light up the skies.

Slide and glide, don't miss the beat,
In this current, feel the heat.
Switch it up, let laughter flow,
Energy's our favorite show.

Spectrum of the Soul

Through the colors, laughter streams,
Each hue bursting with funny themes.
From a giggle to a roar,
A vibrant laugh, forevermore.

In the rainbow of our play,
Every shade a bright bouquet.
Wit ignites like sunbeams' kiss,
Painting moments filled with bliss.

Dancing shadows twist and sway,
In a kaleidoscope display.
Every laugh, a brushstroke bold,
We paint our lives with tales retold.

As colors mix and blend with glee,
Illuminate our jubilee.
In this spectrum, let us find,
The joyful dance of heart and mind.

Electron Dreams

In a lab of light and gleam,
Atoms dance, a wild dream.
Tiny tricks on fluid beams,
Jokes collide like playful schemes.

Electrons in a zany race,
Goofing off at rapid pace.
Wobbling tricks, a silly chase,
Their laughter fills the empty space.

Neutrons roll their eyes in glee,
While protons laugh hysterically.
A subatomic comedy,
In the void, a jubilee.

Lights flicker with a whimsical spark,
Nature's jokes leave a playful mark.
In the quantum realm, we embark,
To find the quirks within the dark.

Brilliance Unbound

In a world where photons play,
Shining bright like a cabaret.
Giggles bounce in every ray,
Lighthearted energy on display.

Color bursts in vivid hues,
A jester's palette, bright and_news.
As particles wiggle, dance and choose,
They crack jokes with no excuse.

Wisps of laughter swirl and spin,
Creating ripples, a playful grin.
In the cosmos, the fun begins,
Where every joke is a win-win!

With quarks and leptons making sound,
In this circus, joy is found.
Science and humor, intertwound,
In the universe, we are all unbound.

Spark of Imagination

A flicker here, a spark in space,
Creativity finds its place.
Ideas bounce with a silly face,
In the chaos, an endless chase.

Witty fusions, laughter's blend,
In every curve, the rules we bend.
From silly sparks, the ideas send,
An electric shock, we gladly spend.

Neurons firing, giggles flow,
Connections made that steal the show.
Imagination's vibrant glow,
Turns the mundane into the flow.

With each thought, we light the way,
Creating fun in every play.
In this realm, we laugh and sway,
A spark of joy, come what may.

Radiance of Truth

In a world of gleaming light,
Truth shines ever so bright.
Its laughter echoes, pure delight,
Unraveling mystery with a bite.

Peering through a prism's dance,
Every hue brings forth a chance.
To giggle at the cosmic glance,
As facts and fun begin to prance.

With every truth, a quirk in tow,
Witty tales that ebb and flow.
In this realm, mischief will grow,
Turning wisdom into a show.

As stars wink with knowing glee,
The universe laughs back at thee.
In brilliance bright, we all agree,
Truth and humor will forever be.

Currents of Emotion

In the rivers of giggles, we float with glee,
Dodging the tickles of a playful spree.
Waves of laughter crash, oh what a sight,
Making every moment feel perfectly right.

Bubbles of joy pop in midair,
Who knew that life could be so rare?
Riding the currents, with friends so near,
Every splash echoes a chorus of cheer.

A whirlpool of worries spins away,
As we prance and dance, come what may.
The skits of the day require no script,
In this sea of happy, we're all well-equipped.

So let's paddle through this buoyant tide,
With silly faces, we take it all in stride.
Because a chuckle shared is the best of all,
In the currents of emotion, we stand tall.

Shimmers of the Mind

In a world of blinks, thoughts shimmer bright,
Ideas twinkle like stars in the night.
Nonsense dances with brilliant obsession,
Every wacky notion, a fun confession.

Gleams of memory, a chatty parade,
Wiggling crayons in a colorful charade.
Dreams like glitter float on the breeze,
Tickling our brains, they aim to please.

Jokes spark and sizzle, like popcorn in heat,
Errant thoughts trip, a comical feat.
Mind's eye winks at the oddest delights,
Unraveling ribbons on whimsical nights.

So let's celebrate with a silly cheer,
For the shimmers that come when friends draw near.
In laughter and whimsy, our thoughts intertwine,
Creating a tapestry that's simply divine.

Language of Light

Words bounce like photons in a goofy spree,
Chasing rainbows, oh what a sight to see!
Every phrase flickers, a flamboyant dance,
Twirling and swirling in a brilliant romance.

Bright beams of puns dart across the floor,
With laughter as bright as a starry decor.
Jokes and jests shine through the fog,
Illuminating paths like a friendly dog.

Tongues twist and turn, a joyous parade,
Glowing with phrases that never will fade.
A luminous lexicon flies through the night,
In this shining world, everything feels right.

So let's light up the stage with words that play,
Chasing shadows, we laugh all day.
In this radiant realm, we're never alone,
For in the language of light, we've made our home.

Twists of Energy

Zipping around like electrons in flight,
Energy sparkles, oh what a delight!
Circuitry giggles, makes us all cheer,
Wires entwined in a playful veneer.

Jumps and jolts of quirky delight,
Bouncing about from morning till night.
Kites of excitement fly high in the air,
As silly shenanigans spark everywhere.

A whirl of motion, a zap and a zoom,
Radiant laughter fills up the room.
Each twist and turn, a quirky surprise,
In the energy dance, our spirits rise.

So let's harness the fun, unleash the charge,
As we whirl through the day, living large.
In the twists of energy, joy is the key,
For every little giggle sets our spirits free.

The Frequency of Heartbeats

In a world of jiggly beats,
Hearts jump like clowns on street.
A rhythm that's quite absurd,
Dancing to a wobbly word.

With every thump and every sway,
We laugh and chuckle, come what may.
Skip a beat, then double-time,
Like a squirrel's acrobatic rhyme.

Glancing at the clock so wide,
Is it ticking, or is it fried?
Laughter echoes through the air,
As we twirl without a care.

Chasing Electric Shadows

Flickering lights in the dark,
Shadows dance like a playful lark.
We run from sparks and little zaps,
Playing tag with goofy flaps.

"Catch me if you can," it squeaks,
Electric giggles, cheeky peeks.
Zap! One's caught, what a surprise,
Laughter lighting up our eyes!

Underneath an electric sky,
We hop like frogs that learned to fly.
Shadows giggle, twirl, and swirl,
In this dance, we laugh and whirl.

Neon Reverie

In a dream of neon lights,
We bounce like rubber with delight.
Colors pop like candy dreams,
Stepping over giggly beams.

A bright blue cat jumps high and quick,
Hilarious twists with each flick.
In this land of glowing hues,
We wear the laughter like our shoes.

Dive into the magenta sea,
Where jellyfish sing joyfully.
In neon waves, we float and sway,
Capturing giggles all the way.

Temporal Sparks

In a whirlwind of time so swift,
Sparks fly like a birthday gift.
We twist and turn with every tick,
Laughter lands like a comical flick.

Time travel's more like a wild chase,
We stumble, giggle, in every place.
Past and future mingle and play,
As we hop through our own ballet.

A portal opens, what a sight!
Where chickens wear hats, oh what a fright!
With every spark, a joke unfurls,
In this dance of whimsical whirls.

The Dance of Particles

In a world where particles twirl,
Electrons giggle, like a swirl.
Neutrons bounce, and protons play,
In this atomic cabaret!

Around they go, a crazy spree,
Bumping into each other, whee!
Silly photons join the song,
Making light beams dance along.

They spin, they twist, they orbit fast,
A scientific party unsurpassed.
With tiny hats and tiny shoes,
They jive and giggle, share their views.

In every atom, joy ignites,
A funny dance of day and nights.
So when you see a flash of light,
Remember, they're dancing, oh what a sight!

Channels of Light

In channels bright, the photons race,
Through prisms bright, they find their place.
They giggle as they bend and show,
Rainbows spring up, and colors glow.

"Look at me," a red ray shouts,
"Now I'm green!" a blue one doubts.
In every hue, they start to tease,
All while dancing with the breeze.

They twist through walls, a playful spree,
"Catch me if you can!" says glee.
In every crevice, light will cheer,
With jokes and jests, they persevere.

Their bright parade lights up the night,
As photons laugh in sheer delight.
So in the dark, remember right,
There's humor hiding in the light!

Eco of the Void

In the void where silence plays,
Echoes giggle in funny ways.
A cosmic whisper, soft and sly,
Jokes that float, oh my, oh my!

"Is anyone there?" a quasar sings,
"Just me and dark matter, we're kings!"
In the absence, laughter rolls,
Invisible jokes from starry souls.

Through galaxies, echoes zoom,
Filling up the cosmic room.
"Knock, knock!" a neutron exclaims,
"Who's there?" "Just space, with no names!"

The void is filled with quirky shout,
As empty space wonders about.
In this silence, joy's unsealed,
In the vastness, fun revealed!

Surging Colors

Colors burst like bubbles high,
Swirling, twirling in the sky.
Red and yellow, blue in tow,
Chasing rainbows, what a show!

With every splash, a jolly cheer,
Colors gather, spreading near.
"Who's the fastest?" green does shout,
"Catch me if you can," no doubt!

They frolic through the morning mist,
Painting sunrises in a twist.
An artist's palette comes alive,
In every shade, they jump and dive.

So when you see a splash so bright,
Know that colors are taking flight.
Laughing hues in a playful race,
Fun and joy in every space!

Vortex of Dreams

Twists and whirls in neon light,
Chasing visions, oh what a sight!
Bouncing thoughts like rubber balls,
In this spiral, laughter calls.

Spin around, a dizzy spree,
Where socks and hats just want to flee!
Dreams collide in a whirlpool fun,
Can we dance, or are we done?

Wobbling minds, they twist and twirl,
In this cyclone, we all swirl!
Floating thoughts take flight, oh dear!
Dreams are wild, but who brought the beer?

Round and round, a mischief spree,
Twisted fate, oh, let it be!
In this vortex, laughter's found,
Where joy and chaos spin around.

Energy in Motion

Jumping jacks of cosmic cheer,
Bouncing high, no need for fear!
Electric vibes, we zigzag fast,
Like a prank that's built to last.

Shuffle here, then slide on by,
With zap and zing, we touch the sky!
Who knew currents could be this fun?
Dancing sparkles, everyone!

Zooming round with giggles bright,
Charged up hugs that feel so right!
What a rush, let's feel the thrill,
As we jet and spin at will!

Energy flows and twists, oh yes!
Chaos in a happy mess!
Let's bounce until the sun goes down,
In this wild electric town.

Chromatic Streams

Colors splash in vibrant flows,
A rainbow dance, where laughter grows!
Swirling hues, with every beam,
Join the fun—just hear them scream!

Splatters here and drips there,
What a sight, beyond compare!
Who spilled paint on the unicorn?
Colors sing, they're never torn!

Mix and blend, a palette true,
Drawing smiles, and giggles too!
A spectrum of joy, we can't outshine,
In this splishy-splashy line!

Chromatic streams, so bold and bright,
What a wild, colorful sight!
Let's splash around and make a mess,
With hues of laughter, we are blessed!

The Dance of Charged Souls

Energy pulses, wiggle and sway,
Charged up souls, we dance all day!
With silly moves and laughter loud,
We twirl and giggle, proud and unbowed.

Jumping jacks with a twisty flair,
Electric vibes are in the air!
Charge your laughs, don't hold it back,
In this dance, we've found our knack!

Spin like a whirlwind, round and round,
With each zap, we've all unbound!
Charged and dancing, what a delight,
Electric smiles shine so bright!

In this wild whirl, we all unite,
Cackling chaos feels so right!
Take my hand, let's stomp and roll,
In the jittery dance of charged soul.

Ionized Spirits

In a lab, the liquids dance,
Atoms swaying, take a chance.
Bubbling beakers, giggles rise,
Einstein chuckles, oh, what a surprise!

Electrons jump, they twist and twirl,
In wild parties, they leap and whirl.
A zap of static, sparks fly high,
Even photons want to join and try!

Bubbles popping, bright and loud,
Chemistry's circus draws a crowd.
With every zap, a brand new cheer,
Won't you join? The fun is near!

Just don't ask why the beakers smile,
We're out here dancing all the while.
A mix of science with a wink,
Who knew reactions could make you think!

Glowing Frequencies

In the dark, they giggle bright,
Frequencies twinkling, oh, what a sight.
Colors flashing, shades collide,
As they hop and dance with pride.

Violet beams and orange rays,
Laughing through the spectral maze.
Doppler shifts make them sway,
"Catch me if you can!" they play!

A rainbow party, who will win?
Invisible tickles on the skin.
Sonic waves just can't sit still,
Creating joy with every thrill!

Let's tune in to the cosmic song,
Where wavelengths pulse and hum along.
A symphony of giggles glows,
We are the music, and it shows!

Bright Horizons

On the edge of dawn's embrace,
Hues of happiness light the space.
A canvas splashed, from pink to blue,
Sunrise laughs, a playful hue.

Particles prance by morning's glow,
Chasing shadows to and fro.
As colors stretch across the sky,
Nature's palette likes to fly!

With giggles high, the clouds parade,
Whispers of humor serenade.
The sun's shy smile peeks out wide,
Tomorrow's fun is set to ride!

So grab a brush and join the fun,
Blend your colors, everyone!
With bright horizons calling near,
Life's a canvas, let's all cheer!

Waves of Color

Surfing on a spectrum wave,
Riding colors that misbehave.
Tangerine and emerald glide,
Tickled fancies side by side.

When violet crashes into gold,
The fun ensues, watch it unfold.
Splashes bright, the laughter flows,
Colors mingle, anything goes!

A color wheel that spins in glee,
Mixing shades with phantasy.
Each wave crashes, tickles the shore,
Who knew a spectrum could be so core?

So laugh aloud on color's crest,
Bellyflops and giggles, we're blessed.
Let's create a riot, bright and bold,
With every hue, let stories unfold!

Arcane Light

In a room where shadows prance,
A bulb flickers, takes a chance,
Juggling light like a clown,
While spaghetti noodles fall down.

Curly wires twist and shout,
A dance-off with a stray cat out,
The toaster sings a funky tune,
As bread does an acrobatic swoon.

Light bulbs pop like champagne corks,
Jazz hands wave from all the forks,
The carpet hums a happy song,
And even the fridge hums along.

With giggles bright, the lamps conspire,
Chasing laughter, raising fire,
In this circus of delight—
Who knew a plug could be so bright!

Surges of Creativity

Colors splatter, paint on walls,
Doodles jump like bouncing balls,
The canvas winks with a grin,
As sticky notes play violin.

Imagination's wild parade,
From paper planes that won't cascade,
Glue sticks dance in a conga line,
As crayons get their groove divine.

Bubbles rise from bubbling ink,
Ideas whirl in a joyful blink,
Muses wear hats made of cheese,
While forgotten socks take their ease.

In chaos, brilliance starts to bloom,
As laughter fills the crowded room,
Creativity, a vibrant wave,
Where every goof is bold and brave!

Resonant Visions

Through the lens, the world is odd,
A chicken dances, smartly trod,
Socks and sandals, quite the look,
A treasure map within a book.

Bouncing bubbles in the air,
Fish on scooters, everywhere,
Kites that giggle as they soar,
And pineapples knock on the door.

Triangles sing their silly songs,
While rectangles chant along,
A pie chart claims it's quite the king,
While polka dots start doing the swing.

In this realm of wacky sights,
Visions sparkle, causing delights,
Each cackle of whimsy seems,
To echo laughter in our dreams!

Kaleidoscopic Rhythms

In a world that twists and spins,
Colors clash, a dance begins,
Lemonade and pickle juice,
They tango, oh, what a loose moose!

Jellybeans stomp to the beat,
Marshmallows shake, oh so sweet,
While pickles strum on funky guitars,
And candy canes crawl to the stars.

With gumballs rolling down the street,
Twirling tops bring the heat,
Cereal sings its crunchy charm,
While licorice draws in a calm.

Rhythms burst in a candy swirl,
As laughter makes the colors twirl,
In this dance of joy and cheer,
We'll boogie-woogie without fear!

Whispers of Energy

In the lab, sparks fly high,
Bottles bubble, oh my my!
Electrons dance, they tiptoe round,
While giggles echo, science-bound.

Flasks filled with fizzy glee,
Reacting as if they were free!
A mix of colors, bright and bold,
Chemistry's secrets, humor told.

Beakers bouncing, silly sights,
Imagine atoms having fights!
They throw their protons, all in jest,
While laughing compounds pass the test.

So here we swirl, a playful blend,
Of quirks and quirks that never end!
With every experiment, we find,
A vibrant laugh that's one of a kind.

Infinity in Color

In a world of hues that wink and sway,
Colors buzzing, in their own play.
A blue wave crashes, then mellows green,
Sunset blushes, a riotous scene.

Like rainbows giggling, stretching wide,
They paint the sky, oh, what a ride!
Crayons arguing, who's the best,
While jellybeans jump, a sugary fest.

The spectrum bounces, skips with glee,
As laughter echoes through the marquee.
A canvas filled with humor bright,
Infinity's joke in pure daylight.

So let's splash colors, joyfully shout,
In this colorful realm, there's never doubt!
Embrace the funny, the silly delight,
Where all the colors dance in flight.

Electromagnetic Essence

Charged particles with a sense of flair,
They swirl and twirl in electric air.
Photons giggle, racing through space,
While electrons join the silly chase.

Bouncing beams, like kids at play,
Watt's the joke? They shout hooray!
Two magnets clash, sparks do ignite,
Magnetic chaos? What a sight!

With static cling, they make a scene,
Hair standing up like a wild teen!
As fields of force make everything sway,
A funny dance in a scientific ballet.

Harness that humor, blend it with might,
For in this world of charge, there's delight!
Laughter waves, a current so strong,
In this essence of fun, we all belong.

Fields of Light

In fields where photons freely roam,
A disco party finds its home.
Twinkling lights that twirl about,
They tease the shadows, laugh, and shout.

Fractal patterns, sparkly bright,
Chasing beams of pure delight.
The sun winks down, a cheeky grin,
As starry friends begin to spin.

Lightning bugs join in the fun,
Glowing brightly, each a pun!
They flicker jokes as they take flight,
In this joyous field of light.

So let's dance under the electric sky,
With laughter echoing, oh so high!
In fields of brightness, we take our place,
Celebrating humor, time, and space.

Neon Dreams

In a world where light's a tease,
Colors dance with such a breeze,
Jellybeans in space take flight,
Wobbling stars bring pure delight.

Cotton candy clouds above,
Bouncing on a moonlit love,
Giggles swirl in every shade,
In this neon world we made.

Lollipop skies with chewy trails,
Electric giggles fill the gales,
Chasing shadows, zipping past,
Life's a joke that will not last.

But in this laugh, we find our spark,
Colorful chaos in the dark,
A blur of fun, we shall embrace,
In the rush of this wild space.

Vibrant Vortices

Whirling winds of candy hues,
Spinning tales of bright reviews,
A taffy twist in every turn,
Where giggles spark and laughter burns.

Jumping jellies, bouncing high,
Riding rainbows in the sky,
Ticklish winds, a swirl so bold,
In vibrant funnels, joy unfolds.

Zany whirlpools, round and round,
Tickling toes and laughter sound,
Frantic frolics take the stage,
In this theater of pure rage.

So grab a friend and join the ride,
On color wheels, let's slip and slide,
In vibrant realms where fun won't cease,
We'll dance our way to sweet release.

Radiant Echoes

Echoes of laughter bounce and play,
In a kaleidoscope where silliness stays,
Bouncing beats of joy unfold,
Whimsical whispers, stories told.

Giggles echo in bright delight,
Chasing shadows through the night,
Sparkling dreams in every sound,
In this chorus, joy is found.

Round and round, like spinning tops,
Nonsensical tales, the fun never stops,
Tickling echoes in every room,
Filling the air, a bubbly bloom.

So let your heart join in the cheer,
Celebrate the joy we hold dear,
With radiant echoes, we shall rise,
In laughter's glow, we touch the skies.

Charged Verses

Charged with whimsy, words collide,
Sparky topics we can't hide,
Like lightning bugs on silly flights,
Filling our nights with quirky sights.

Rumbling giggles, buzzing loud,
Tickling fancies, feeling proud,
Wacky phrases, zany joy,
In this jolt, we leap and buoy.

Shocking tales with a funny twist,
In vibrant realms, we can't resist,
Bizarre antics on parade,
Crafting giggles that won't fade.

So grab a quirk and hold on tight,
In charged verses, we take flight,
A wild ride through laughter's lands,
Join the fun, let's make some plans!

Resonating Waves

In the ocean of giggles, we float with ease,
Tickling the surface, riding the breeze.
Splashing with laughter, we dive and we soar,
Waves of delight, always wanting more.

Jellyfish dance in a wobbly line,
Each jiggle and jive, oh, what a sign!
Bubbles erupt with a pop and a plop,
In this sea of chuckles, we never stop.

Seagulls join in with their honks and their squawks,
As we surf on the silliness, swaying like stalks.
The tide pulls us closer, we twirl and we sway,
In this wacky water, we play all day.

So grab your floaties, let the fun unfold,
In these waves of joy, we're never too old.
Riding the crest of a giggle parade,
Laughing together, no chance to fade.

Cosmic Threads

Stitching the stars with a needle of light,
Crafting a blanket of giggles so bright.
Each twinkle a pun, each planet a joke,
In this cosmic quilt, we happily soak.

The moon winks at us, as we thread and we weave,
Telling us tales that we can't quite believe.
Shooting stars zoom by, with a wink and a grin,
Sprinkling confetti where the fun will begin.

Galaxies twist in their fanciful dance,
While comets burst forth, igniting our chance.
Together we laugh at the chaos we see,
In the fabric of space, forever carefree.

So grab a star and spin it around,
In this cosmic playground, silliness found.
With threads of delight, let's patch up our day,
In this universe of funny, we'll play!

Shimmering Reflections

Mirrors of laughter gloss over our frowns,
Showing us selfies with silly clown gowns.
Each wink and each giggle, a sparkle in view,
In this world of reflections, joy's never through.

The puddles below play tricks with their shine,
As we leap and we splash, like a dance in divine.
Catching the whimsy of moments gone by,
Each ripple a chuckle that can't help but fly.

We dance with our shadows, they shimmy and sway,
In this funhouse of mirrors, we're wild and we play.
Twisting all images into delight,
What once was a frown is now pure starlight!

So let's tiptoe, let's skip, and let's grin wide,
In this shimmering world, we have nothing to hide.
With reflections of joy, we'll sparkle and glow,
A dance of existence, laughter in tow.

The Glow of Existence

Under the sun's gaze, we bask and we beam,
Radiating laughter, the ultimate dream.
With every beam bright, we shine and we sway,
Creating a glow that brightens the day.

Fireflies twinkle, like stars gone astray,
Chasing each other in a wiggly play.
While daisies laugh softly, a giggle, a cheer,
In this garden of joy, all spirits adhere.

We bounce on the grass, each leap is a giggle,
The sun's ray tickles, makes everyone wriggle.
Swaying like flowers, we dance in the breeze,
Where joy blooms eternal, just as we please.

So let's glow with the fun, let's brighten the night,
In this tapestry woven with laughter so bright.
With smiles as our lanterns, we light up the scene,
In the glow of existence, we dance and we preen.

Celestial Conduits

In space where the starlight plays,
A comet sneezes, bright it razes.
Planets giggle, twirl about,
While rockets dance, there's no doubt.

Asteroids are just floating rocks,
Wearing hats, doing silly talks.
Galaxies swirl in a waltz,
Creating laughter, no faults.

Fragments of Aurora

The sky wears a coat of neon hues,
Making whimsical shapes, a playful muse.
Each shimmer winks, a joke to share,
While shooting stars do silly flair.

The colors chuckle, twist and spin,
Like jellybeans on a sugar binge.
Catch a light wave, hold it tight,
For the next giggle comes with night.

Electromagnetic Heart

A circuit sings with a zany tune,
As wires twist like a wiggly worm.
With every pulse, it plays a part,
In this quirky, buzzing heart.

The sparks shoot out, a lightning grin,
Twirling chaotically, it pulls you in.
Catch the beat, feel that spark,
In the dance of light, don't lose your mark.

Flowing Frequencies

Waves are laughing as they glide,
Surfing on the sound tide.
Tickling air with squeaky sounds,
Bouncing joy, it knows no bounds.

Whispers giggle in every tone,
As echoes dance in happy moan.
Tuned to fun, they sway and sway,
Riding laughter all the way.

Luminous Thoughts

Bright ideas bounce around,
Like fireflies in the night,
They dance on silly wings,
With laughter taking flight.

In every mind they spark,
A glow beneath the skin,
Connecting like a circuit,
Where silliness begins.

They flicker and they flash,
In colors oh so bold,
A rainbow made of giggles,
Like stories yet untold.

With each bright bulb that shines,
A joke comes to the fore,
A luminary spirit,
Who can resist some more?

Streams of Connection

Wires crossed and tangled up,
With humor we can meet,
Like two birds on a wire,
Making melodies sweet.

A giggle flowing freely,
Between the lines we draw,
These streams of silly banter,
Such cackles with no flaw.

In currents filled with joy,
We ride the waves of cheer,
With every witty quip,
We draw the laughter near.

Electricity of minds,
A shock that sparks delight,
In every tossed-out punchline,
We find our shared insight.

Radiant Vibes

The room's alive with laughter,
As jokes just take their toll,
A vibe that lifts the spirits,
Like laughter's perfect goal.

With every little chuckle,
The air is bright and fun,
Who knew the hum of joy
Could shine like morning sun?

Bouncing off the walls,
Like colors in a swirl,
It's comedy in motion,
To make the laughter twirl.

Potent waves of humor,
Zapping into minds,
A radiant connection,
Where every heart it finds.

Energy as Emotion

Feelings zip like lightning,
In storms of pure delight,
Emotions burst like bubbles,
In laughter's warm sunlight.

The charge of every giggle,
An electric little spark,
Igniting every moment,
A flame that leaves its mark.

Shocking all the senses,
With jests that tickle pink,
This energy of humor,
Allows us all to think.

In this crazy whirlwind,
Of joy beyond compare,
We find our goofy essence,
And leave behind the care.

www.ingramcontent.com/pod-product-compliance
Lightning Source LLC
Chambersburg PA
CBHW071850160426
43209CB00003B/490